AMERICAN CURRENCY

MONEY

Patricia Armentrout

The Rourke Press, Inc.
Vero Beach, Florida 32964

PHOTO CREDITS
© Armentrout: pg. 8; © Corel Corporation: Cover, pgs. 4, 10, 15,
18; © Department of the Treasury Bureau of Engraving and
Printing: pg. 21; © East Coast Studios: pg 13, 17; © East Coast
Studios: Title page, pg. 12; © The Smithsonian Institution National
Numismatic Collection: pg. 7

ACKNOWLEDGMENTS
The author acknowledges David Armentrout for his contribution in
writing this book.

Library of Congress Cataloging-in-Publication Data

Armentrout, Patricia, 1960 -
    American Currency / by Patricia Armentrout
        p. cm. — (Money)
    Includes index.
    Summary: An introduction to the characteristics and values of
the different coins and paper money used as currency in the
United States.
    ISBN 1-57103-122-7
    1. Money—United States—Juvenile literature.
2. Coins—United States—Juvenile literature. 3. Paper money—
United States—Juvenile literature. [1. Money. 2. Coins.]
I. Title II. Series: Armentrout, Patricia, 1960 -   Money.
HG221.5.A687 1996
332.4' 973—dc20   96–3458
                                                   CIP
                                                   AC

Printed in the USA

TABLE OF CONTENTS

CURRENCY

Imagine how hard it would be to buy or sell something if everyone used a different kind of money. How would you know how much your money was worth?

To solve this problem, we use a standard type of money called **currency** (KER en see). Currency is cash and is used to pay for goods and services.

Coins and paper money are the two types of currency, and each is made in standard **values** (VAL yooz).

THE FIRST AMERICAN PAPER MONEY

The Continental Congress, our country's first government, made money to help pay for its war against Great Britain. The paper money, or notes, were called **continentals** (KAHN te NEN tulz).

The value, or worth, of the notes was backed by silver and gold. When silver and gold became scarce, the continentals became worthless.

The government was more successful making coins at the first U. S. **Mint** (MINT) in Philadelphia. The precious metals used in the new coins guaranteed their value.

Early American currency issued in 1776

EIGHTEEN PENCE

1/6   1/6

No.

EIGHTEEN PENCE,

According to the RESOLVES of the ASSEMBLY of PENNSYLVANIA, of the 6th Day of April, in the 16th Year of the Reign of His Majesty GEO. the Third. Dated at Philadelphia, the 25th Day of APRIL, Anno Domini 1776.

1s6d   1s6d

UNITED STATES MONEY

American people no longer depend on gold or silver to back their money's value. Instead the U. S. government guarantees the value of money.

United States money is based on the dollar. The dollar is worth 100 cents. The dollar is paper money called a bill. Bills are printed in many values greater than 100 cents.

On every bill these words are printed: "This note is legal tender..." The term "legal tender" means the dollar has value and must be accepted as payment for goods and services.

BY THE NUMBERS

When you look at a coin or bill, you will see several markings. Numbers are used on all United States currency, but more numbers are on bills than coins.

The large number printed on the corners of the face side of a bill shows the value. A serial number gives each bill its own identity. You will also find the year the bill was printed.

The only numbers found on a coin show the year the coin was made.

The value of these bills is shown by the number printed in the corners

Schools need money to buy computers and other equipment and supplies

Construction work is just one of many ways to earn money

WORDS ON MONEY

Words on United States money identify portraits, American symbols, and the value of the currency.

The word "Liberty" is stamped on all U. S. coins to show how important freedom is to Americans. The motto "In God We Trust" appears on all currency since 1984.

The Latin phrase "E pluribus unum" is used on most money. The words mean "out of many, one." The phrase is important because the U. S. is made up of people from all over the world.

The portrait of George Washington, the first U. S. President, is on the U. S. one-dollar bill and the quarter

HEADS

If you have ever seen a coin tossed at a football game, then you may know the expression "heads or tails."

The head, or front side of a coin, is the side with the portrait. A portrait of a famous American appears on all United States currency.

The Secretary of the U. S. Treasury chooses the designs and portraits. Portraits cannot be of a living person. With some exceptions, portraits on currency honor past U. S. presidents.

1. Front and back of penny
2. Front and back of nickel
3. Front and back of dime
4. Front and back of quarter

1

2

3

4

TAILS

The tail, or back, side of United States money usually displays an American symbol. The back of some coins show historic places. Thomas Jefferson's home is on the back of the nickel. The Lincoln Memorial is on the back of the penny.

Since paper money is printed, the designs on it can be more detailed than on coins, which are minted. For example, compare the Lincoln Memorial on the back of a five dollar bill with the one on the back of a penny.

The Lincoln Memorial honors our 16th president and welcomes people inside to the museum

MONEY FACTS

United States paper money, or bills, are printed in values of 1, 5, 10, 20, 50, and 100 dollars. At one time 5,000 and 10,000 dollar bills were printed and used by banks.

Money **circulates** (SER kyoo LATES), or changes hands, every day to pay for products and services. An average bill lasts only about 16 months.

The Denver Mint produces one million coins an hour! Most coins are in circulation for over 15 years.

Crisp new $50 bills rolling off a printing press

AMERICA'S CHANGING MONEY

United States law states that the designs of U. S. coins can be changed only once in 25 years.

New coins are made now and then. Not all new coins are accepted by the people. The Susan B. Anthony dollar coin, issued in 1979, is an example. People did not use it because of its size. The coin was often confused with the quarter. The mint stopped producing the coin in 1981.

Paper money designs change too. In 1990 changes were made to paper currency to make it harder to **counterfeit** (KOUN ter FIT), or copy illegally.

Glossary

circulates (SER kyoo LATES) — passes from one place to another

continentals (KAHN te NEN tulz) — the first paper money issued by the Continental Congress

counterfeit (KOUN ter FIT) — to copy; a fake or forgery

currency (KER en see) — money

mint (MINT) — a place where coins are made; to make coins

value (VAL yoo) — the amount of money something is worth or the fair exchange for something

INDEX